Notes to self...

Notes to self...

Notes to self...

Notes to self...

Notes to self...

Notes to self...

Notes to self...

Notes to self...

Notes to self...

Notes to self...

Notes to self...

Notes to self...

Notes to self...

Notes to self...

Notes to self...

Notes to self...

Notes to self...

Notes to self...

Notes to self...

Notes to self...

Notes to self...

Notes to self...

Notes to self...

Notes to self...

Notes to self...

Notes to self...

Notes to self...

Notes to self...

Notes to self...

Notes to self...

Notes to self...

Notes to self...

Notes to self...

Notes to self...

Notes to self...

Notes to self...

Notes to self...

Notes to self...

Notes to self...

Notes to self...

Notes to self...

Notes to self...

Notes to self...

Notes to self...

Notes to self...

Notes to self...

Notes to self...

Notes to self...

Notes to self...

Notes to self...

Notes to self...

Notes to self...

Notes to self...

Notes to self...

Notes to self...

Notes to self...

Notes to self...

Notes to self...

Notes to self...

Notes to self...

Notes to self...

Notes to self...

Notes to self...

Notes to self...

Notes to self...

Notes to self...

Notes to self...

Notes to self...

Notes to self...

Notes to self...

Notes to self...

Notes to self...

Notes to self...

Notes to self...

Notes to self...

Notes to self...

Notes to self...

Notes to self...

Notes to self...

Notes to self...

Notes to self...

Notes to self...

Notes to self...

Notes to self...

Notes to self...

Notes to self...

Notes to self...

Notes to self...

Notes to self...

Notes to self...

Notes to self...

Notes to self...

Notes to self...

Notes to self...

Notes to self...

Notes to self...

Notes to self...

Notes to self...

Notes to self...

Notes to self...

www.ingramcontent.com/pod-product-compliance
Lightning Source LLC
Chambersburg PA
CBHW020552220526
45463CB00006B/2275